CHRISTMAS TREATS

INSPIRATIONAL IDEAS FOR DECORATIVE
AND EDIBLE GIFTS

LORENZ BOOKS

LONDON • NEW YORK • SYDNEY • BATH

This edition published in the UK in 1997 by Lorenz Books

© Anness Publishing Limited 1997

Lorenz Books is an imprint of
Anness Publishing Limited
Hermes House
88-89 Blackfriars Road
London SE1 8HA

ISBN 1 85967 547 6

A CIP catalogue record for this book is available from the British Library

Publisher: Joanna Lorenz
Project Editor: Fiona Eaton
Designer: Lilian Lindblom
Jacket Designer: Harriet Athay
Illustrations: Anna Koska

Printed and bound in China

1 3 5 7 9 10 8 6 4 2

*For all recipes, quantities are given in both metric and imperial measures, and, where
appropriate, measures are also given in standard cups and spoons. Follow one set, but not a
mixture, because they are not interchangeable.*

Contents

Introduction

The weeks leading up to Christmas can be a period of frantic activity, but they can also be exciting and satisfying if you give some time and thought to the lovely things you can create to make your own Christmas extra special.

This is an unrivalled opportunity to give free rein to your creativity as you decorate your home and plan your table. Lighten the dark days of winter with the glint of gold, the enchanting glow of candlelight and the scent of freshly gathered evergreens. The craft ideas in this book will set you thinking and help you to enrich the festive scene.

Everyone loves treats at Christmas, particularly edible ones. Even if you do not have time to make your own sweets (candies), chocolates, cookies or preserves during the rest of the year, at Christmas it is particularly rewarding to pamper your family and friends with these luxurious and delicious ideas. Serve them at your own table, or pack them carefully in boxes or pretty jars to make perfect gifts.

It is a good idea to start planning your Christmas treats several months earlier. While vegetables and fruit are cheap and plentiful in the autumn, you can turn them into delicious preserves to hoard in your Christmas store.

Home-made potpourri makes a lovely gift, so collect and dry flowers and herbs while they are abundant in your garden. Add to your collection of rich fabrics, gold paper, ribbons and candles all through the year, to make original and beautiful decorations at Christmas. It's a treat to create, as well as give, lovely things, so use these ideas to make preparing for Christmas a time to enjoy.

GILDED FIG PYRAMID

An almost profligate use of figs produces a gloriously decadent decoration for the festive table.
The deep purple figs with their dusting of gold, arranged with geometric precision, create an opulent
yet architectural focal point for the most indulgent Christmas feasts.

MATERIALS

florist's dry foam cone approximately
25 cm (10 in) high
gilded terracotta flowerpot
all-purpose glue
wax gilt
40 black figs
stub (floral) wires
50 ivy leaves

1 Make sure that the dry foam cone sits comfortably in the pot. To ensure that it is stable, put a dab of glue around the edge of the cone base. Gild the figs slightly on one side of the fruit only, by rubbing the wax gilt on to the skin with your fingers.

2 Wire the gilded figs by pushing a stub (floral) wire horizontally through the flesh approximately 2.5 cm (1 in) above the base of the fruit. Carefully bend the two protruding pieces of wire so that they point downwards. Take care not to tear the skin of the figs.

TIP

This display has a powerful impact that is disproportionate to the simplicity of its construction.

3 Attach the figs to the cone by pushing their wires into the dry foam. Work in concentric circles around the cone upwards from the bottom.

4 When you reach the top, position the last fig on the tip of the dry foam cone, with its stem going upwards to create a point.

5 Make hairpin shapes out of the stub (floral) wires and fix the ivy leaves into the cone between the figs, covering any exposed foam.

BLUE PINE CHRISTMAS CANDLE

Lavish quantities of blue pine (spruce) combine with roses and cones in a marvellous Christmas table decoration. Make the arrangement with freshly cut branches so that their perfume can be enjoyed.

MATERIALS

knife
florist's dry foam block
terracotta flowerpot
candle
hay
secateurs (pruning shears)
blue pine (spruce)
stub (floral) wires
reindeer moss
mossing (floral) pins
dried roses
pine cones
kutchi fruit
dried mushrooms

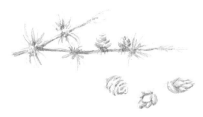

TIP

Never leave a display with a lighted candle burning unattended. When creating a design, always ensure that the dried materials are as far away from the candle as possible.

1 Trim the foam block so that it fits tightly in the pot and fix the candle. Pack any space around the foam with hay. Trim the needles from the base of each blue pine (spruce) stem, to make it easier to insert into the foam. Starting at the base, position the largest pieces so that they lean down slightly.

3 Fill any large spaces in the display with moss, fixing it in place with mossing (floral) pins. Put plenty of moss around the base of the candle, to cover any fixings.

2 Add more of the larger pieces all around the pot. Using shorter lengths, add a layer above the first. Continue until the final and shortest layer is added, nearest to the candle. When adding the smaller pieces, use a stub (floral) wire to give strength or length. Keep the foliage well away from the base of the candle.

4 Wire the roses into bunches. Wire the pine cones, kutchi fruit and dried mushrooms. Add the wired materials, using them to fill any spaces in the foliage.

CHRISTMAS CANDLE TABLE DECORATION

When the table is groaning under the weight of festive fare, complete the picture with a candlelit decoration in seasonal reds and greens. Bright anemones, ranunculus and holly are set off by the grey of lichen on larch (pine) twigs and the soft green of aromatic rosemary. The simple white candles are given a festive lift with their individual bows.

MATERIALS

25 cm (10 in) florist's foam ring
25 cm (10 in) wire basket with candleholders
knife
10 stems rosemary
10 small stems lichen-covered larch (pine)
10 small stems holly
scissors
30 stems red anemones ('Mona Lisa')
30 stems red ranunculus
pleated paper ribbon
4 candles

TIP
Never leave burning candles unattended and do not allow the candles to burn below 5 cm (2 in) above the display.

1 Soak the florist's foam ring in water and wedge it into the wire basket. If you need to trim the ring slightly, make sure that you do not cut too much off – it should fit snugly.

2 Use a combination of rosemary, larch (pine) and holly to create an even but textured foliage and twig outline, all around the foam ring. Make sure that the stems towards the outside of the ring are shorter than those in the centre.

3 Cut the stems of the anemones and ranunculus to 7.5 cm (3 in). Arrange them evenly throughout the display, leaving a little space around the candleholders. Make four ribbon bows and attach them to the candles. Position the candles in the holders.

VELVET STOCKING

This rather grown-up stocking made of rich, dark colours is so grand
that it is just asking to be filled with exquisite treats and presents.

MATERIALS

paper for templates
pencil
pins
gold satin fabric
scissors
tailor's chalk
dress-weight velvet in three
complementary colours
sewing machine
matching sewing thread
decorative braid
sequin ribbon
sewing needle
gold buttons

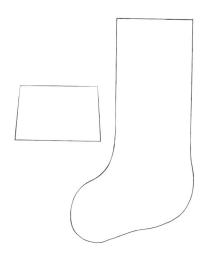

1 Copy the template for the cuff, enlarge to the size required, and cut it out. Pin to a double thickness of gold satin fabric and draw around it with tailor's chalk, leaving a narrow seam allowance. Cut out the pieces.

2 Enlarge the stocking template and divide into three sections. Pin each pattern piece to a double thickness of each colour velvet. Draw around each piece, leaving a narrow seam allowance, and cut out.

3 Pin the three stocking sections together. Then machine stitch the stocking and the gold satin cuff together to make each side of the stocking. On the right side of each piece, pin a strip of decorative braid and sequin ribbon. Sew these on invisibly by hand.

4 With right sides together, stitch the two sides of the stocking and cuff together. Turn through, then fold the satin inside the stocking, leaving a deep cuff. Turn in the raw edge of the cuff, and slip stitch it to the stocking seams. Trim with gold buttons and attach a loop of braid.

WHITE CHRISTMAS TREE

*Stand this abstract, modern interpretation of the traditional star-topped
Christmas tree on a side-table or the mantelpiece. It looks best as part of
a restrained white-and-gold arrangement.*

MATERIALS

*glue gun
coarse sisal string
large polystyrene cone
scissors
small polystyrene star
paintbrushes
white emulsion (latex) paint
gold paint*

1 Using a glue gun, attach the end of the string to the base of the cone. Wind the string up towards the point, then down to the base again, gluing it as you work. Each time you reach the base, cut the string and start again from another point.

2 When you have covered the cone evenly with string, wind a short length into a coil and glue it to the top of the cone to make a stable base for the star to sit on.

3 Wind and glue string around the star in the same way. Hide the raw ends under the star. Glue the star to the top of the cone.

4 Paint the cone and star with several coats of white emulsion (latex) paint, covering the string and filling in any dips in the polystyrene.

5 Finish by brushing roughly over the string with gold paint.

CLASSIC CLOVE & ORANGE POMANDERS

The traditional pomander starts as a fresh orange and dries into a beautiful decoration with a warm spicy smell evocative of mulled wine and the festive season. Several pomanders, tied with different ribbons, make a lovely Christmas gift. They can be displayed together in a bowl, hung up around the house, used as Christmas decorations or put in a wardrobe to scent its contents.

MATERIALS

3 contrasting lengths of ribbon
3 small, firm oranges
cloves
scissors

1 Tie a length of ribbon around each orange as if you were tying it around a parcel. Cross it over at the base and bring the ends up to the top of the orange.

2 Finish off by tying the ribbon into a bow. Adjust the position of the ribbon as necessary to ensure that the orange is divided into four equal-sized sections.

TIP

The oranges will shrink as they dry out so you will probably need to tighten the ribbons and re-tie the bows.

3 Starting at the edges of the sections, push the sharp ends of the cloves into the exposed orange skin and continue until each quarter is completely covered. Trim the ends of the ribbon neatly.

CROSS-STITCH CHRISTMAS TREE DECORATION

*This bright seasonal design of holly and berries will continue to give
pleasure for many Christmases to come. You could set yourself a challenge and
complete a whole set of embroidered decorations.*

MATERIALS

*14 hpi white aida, 13 cm (5 in) square
tapestry needle
stranded embroidery thread (floss) as
listed in key
pencil
tape measure
scissors
sewing needle
matching sewing thread
8 cm (3¼ in) embroidery frame
felt*

1 Following the chart, work the
design using two strands of
embroidery thread (floss) for the
cross-stitch and one strand for the
backstitch. When the design is
complete, draw a 10 cm (4 in) circle
around it and cut it out.

2 Run a double gathering stitch
5 mm (¼ in) inside the raw edge
of the fabric. Position the design over
the inside rim of the embroidery
frame and draw up the gathering
thread, keeping the design in the
centre of the frame.

3 Lace the embroidery into the
back of the frame and replace
the outside ring over the frame.
Finish by slip stitching a circle of felt
over the back.

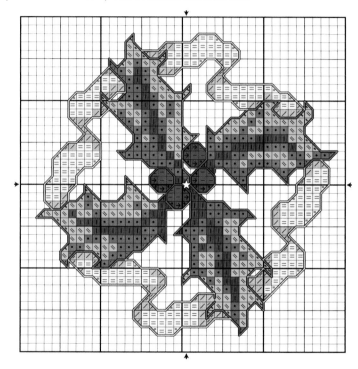

	Cross-stitch in two strands		Backstitch in one strand
⊥⊥	1044 Dark grass green	—	246 Mid grass green
••	246 Mid grass green	=	47 Dark red
◊◊	245 Privet green	=	307 Gold
⇉⇉	47 Dark red		
▬▬	46 Berry red	☆	Middle point
∕∕	307 Gold		
==	298 Deep yellow		The thread numbers refer to Anchor threads.

SPICE DECORATION

*Cinnamon sticks keep their rich, spicy smell for many years, and provide
a perfect base on which to mount other natural decorations. Use any combination
of ribbons, lace, fine chain, gold cord and bells, along with cones,
grasses and seed pods.*

MATERIALS

*long cinnamon sticks
glue gun
selection of bark, cones, seed pods
and dried foliage
narrow red ribbon
gold cord
small bell*

1 Join the cinnamon sticks together to make a staggered raft shape. Use the glue gun to make this base.

2 Stick individual natural decorations on to the base with dabs of glue from the glue gun.

3 Wrap the ribbon around the bundle, crossing it over several times before tying it at the back. Wind the gold cord around the decoration, tie the bell to the end of the cord, and leave the end with the bell hanging down.

HERBAL POTPOURRI

Using dried herbs, you can quickly produce a mixture that will scent the room delightfully.
Give it an occasional stir to release more fragrance.

MATERIALS

1 handful dried mint leaves
2 handfuls dried marigold flowers
1 handful any other dried herbs, such
as thyme, sage or marjoram
10 dried orange slices
6 cinnamon sticks
a few dried chillies
4 nutmegs
5 ml (1 tsp) mint essential oil
15 ml (1 tbsp) sweet orange
essential oil
mixing bowl
spoon for mixing
large plastic bag
15 ml (1 tbsp) ground orris root

1 Mix all the ingredients, except the orris root, together in the bowl. Make sure the oils are well mixed with all the other ingredients.

2 Tip the mixture into a large plastic bag, add the orris root and shake well. Tie to close. Leave to mature for 1–2 weeks, shaking occasionally. Then tip the mixture into a suitable bowl or dish to display it.

RAFFIA BALLS

To give your Christmas tree a natural look, replace glitzy glass ornaments with these little balls covered in creamy, undyed raffia. Their subtle shade and interesting texture go beautifully with the tree's soft green branches.

MATERIALS

scissors
fine copper wire
small polystyrene balls
double-sided adhesive tape
natural (garden) raffia

TIP

Vary the basic design by using coloured raffia, or glue some dried flowers or cones to the top of the balls.

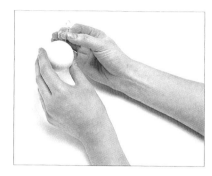

1 Cut a short piece of wire and make it into a loop. Push the ends into a polystyrene ball.

2 Cover the ball completely in double-sided adhesive tape to form a base for the raffia.

3 Arrange the hank of raffia so that you can remove lengths without tangling them. Holding the first 10 cm (4 in) of the strand at the top of the ball, wind the raffia around, working from top to bottom and covering the shape as evenly as possible.

4 When you have finished covering the ball, tie the end of the raffia to the length you left free at the beginning. Using a few strands of raffia together, tie a bow over these two ends to finish off the top of the decoration.

GILDED GLASS SPHERES

*With a gold glass-painting outliner, you can turn plain glass
tree decorations into unique gilded ornaments. Do not be too ambitious
with your designs: you will find that simple repeating motifs such as
circles, triangles and stars can actually be the most effective.*

MATERIALS

*plain glass tree ornaments
detergent
white spirit (paint thinner)
soft cloth
gold glass-painting outliner
paper tissues
jam jar
wire-edged ribbon*

1 Before you begin to apply the
paint, clean the glass thoroughly
with detergent and wipe it with
white spirit (paint thinner) to remove
all traces of grease.

2 Working on one side only,
gently squeeze the gold glass-
painting outliner on to the glass. If
you make a mistake, wipe it off
quickly with a paper tissue while it is
still wet.

3 Rest the sphere on an empty jam
jar and leave for about 24 hours
to dry thoroughly. Decorate the other
side and leave to dry again.

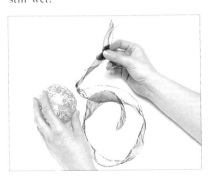

4 Thread a length of wire-edged
ribbon through the loop at the
top of the ornament and tie it in
a decorative bow.

ICE BOX

A great big box under the Christmas tree always attracts attention, but this stunning gift wrap is in danger of upstaging the Christmas tree itself! Plain blue paper is stencilled with snowflakes, then the whole gift is bunched up in clear ice-like cellophane (plastic wrap). Foil ribbons and Christmas tree ornaments complete the effect.

MATERIALS

tracing paper
pencil
thin card (cardboard) or acetate sheet
craft knife
cutting mat
bright blue wrapping paper
small sponge
white watercolour paint
clear adhesive tape
scissors
roll of clear, wide cellophane (plastic wrap)
silver foil ribbon
selection of silver Christmas tree ornaments

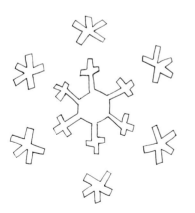

1 Enlarge the snowflake design as required, trace it and transfer it to the card (cardboard) or acetate sheet. Cut out the stencil carefully, using a craft knife and a cutting mat, then lay the stencil over the wrapping paper.

2 Use a small damp sponge to apply the white watercolour paint sparingly through the stencil. Stencil the snowflakes randomly all over the blue paper, continuing over the edges.

3 If necessary, join enough stencilled sheets of wrapping paper with adhesive tape to make one large sheet to wrap the box. Cut a length of cellophane (plastic wrap) long enough to pass under the box and up the sides, with at least 30 cm (12 in) extra on both ends. Do the same in the other direction, to cross over the first sheet under the box.

4 Gather up the cellophane (plastic wrap) on top of the boxed gift, making sure that the sides of the box are completely covered, then bunch the ends close to the box top and tape around them tightly.

5 Cover the adhesive tape with silver foil ribbon and tie in a bow. Trim the ends of the ribbon and attach the tree ornaments.

BOLD RED & GOLD GIFT WRAP

*There is something sumptuous about red tissue paper – the rustling noise
and smooth texture impart a sense of luxury, and the colour deepens with layering.
Stamp the paper with large gold stars and you will have one of the most stunning
gift wraps around.*

MATERIALS

pack of red tissue paper
scrap paper
big star rubber stamp
gold ink
clear adhesive tape
scissors
gold ribbon, cord or tinsel

1 Lay a sheet of red tissue paper on scrap paper and, beginning in one corner, work diagonally across the sheet, stamping gold stars about 5 cm (2 in) apart. Leave to dry.

2 Wrap the gift using a lining of two sheets of plain red tissue paper under the stamped sheet. Use clear adhesive tape to secure the ends.

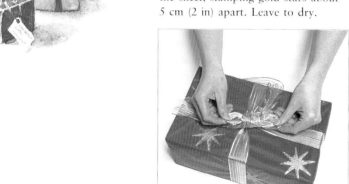

3 Trim the wrapped gift with a gold ribbon, cord or tinsel tied on top in a single bow.

4 To finish, cut the ribbon ends into swallowtails to match the points of the stars.

CHRISTMAS TREE GIFT TAGS

Beautiful hand-made gift tags will add the finishing touch to your carefully wrapped presents. Spend some time making yourself a selection of stamped, stencilled and painted motifs before you begin to assemble the gift tags.

MATERIALS

pencil
cellulose kitchen sponge
scissors
glue stick
corrugated cardboard
stencil paint in gold and black
coloured and textured paper
tracing paper
stencil card (cardboard)
craft knife
cutting mat
white cartridge (heavy) paper
paintbrushes
bright watercolour inks
white oil crayon
brown parcel wrap
metal ruler
thin card (cardboard) in
various colours
hole punch
fine gold cord

1 Draw the Christmas tree motif on the kitchen sponge and cut out carefully to make a positive and a negative image. Glue each stamp to a piece of cardboard. Stamp both motifs in gold on to a selection of papers in different textures and colours (use tracing paper as well).

2 Trace the Christmas tree branch pattern and transfer it to a piece of stencil card (cardboard). Cut out the design using a craft knife. Stencil some branches in black and others in gold on to a selection of different papers and on some of the stamped gold Christmas tree motifs.

3 Paint plain white cartridge (heavy) paper with watercolour ink in bright, vivid colours and then cut simple star motifs from the different colours.

4 Use a white oil crayon to scribble spots on brown parcel wrap for snow-flakes. Tear them out individually leaving a border of brown paper.

5 Using a craft knife and a metal ruler, cut out tags from thin card (cardboard) in various colours. Cut or tear a selection of motifs, arrange them on the tags and glue down. Punch a hole in the top and thread it with a loop of gold cord.

CHRISTMAS CRACKERS

*Making your own Christmas crackers is really rewarding and it is great fun
watching friends and family pull them open to discover the treats inside.*

MATERIALS

*double-sided crêpe paper in
bright colours
craft knife
metal ruler
cutting mat
double-sided adhesive tape
thin card (cardboard) in
white and black
gold crêpe paper
gold paper-backed foil
corrugated cardboard
fine gold cord
cracker snaps
paper hats, jokes and gifts
narrow black ribbon*

3 Decorate the cracker with
strips of the gold paper. Lay a
strip of paper-backed foil over a
piece of corrugated cardboard and
ease the foil into the ridges. Cut a
star shape out of thin black card
(cardboard), wrap fine gold cord
around it and stick it on the cracker.

1 For each cracker, cut two
25 x 20 cm (10 x 8 in) rectangles
of crêpe paper. Join, overlapping the
ends, to make 45 x 20 cm (18 x 8 in)
sheets. Cut three pieces of white card
(cardboard) 23 x 10 cm (9 x 4 in).
Roll each into a cylinder, overlapping
the short ends by 3 cm (1¼ in).

4 Insert a cracker snap and place
the novelties in the central
section of the cracker. Tie up the
ends with narrow black ribbon,
easing the crêpe paper gently so that
you can tie the knots very tightly.

2 Lay strips of double-sided
adhesive tape across the crêpe
paper on which to attach the card
cylinders: one in the centre and the
other two about 4 cm (1½ in) in
from each end of the rectangle. Roll
up and secure the edge with double-
sided tape.

5 Complete the cracker by folding
the edges of the crêpe paper over
the ends of the cardboard tubes.
Make as many crackers as you will
need, perhaps varying the colours
and decorations slightly.

GINGERBREAD HOUSE

This gingerbread house makes a memorable family Christmas gift or
party centrepiece, especially if it is filled with lots of little gifts and surprises.

MAKES 1 HOUSE

90 ml (6 tbsp) golden syrup
(corn syrup)
30 ml (2 tbsp) black treacle (molasses)
75 g (3 oz/⅓ cup) soft light
brown sugar
75 g (3 oz/5 tbsp) butter
450 g (1 lb/4 cups) plain flour
15 g (½ oz/1 tbsp) ground ginger
15 g (½ oz/1 tbsp) bicarbonate of soda
(baking soda)
2 egg yolks
225 g (8 oz) barley sugar sweets
(hard candies)

ICING AND DECORATION
royal icing
25 cm (10 in) square silver cake board
icing (confectioners') sugar for dusting
1.5 m (1 ½ yd) ribbon

TIP

Before you make the gingerbread,
cut the following shapes from stiff
card (cardboard): For the side walls:
2 rectangles 15 x 10 cm (6 x 4 in).
For the end walls: 2 rectangles
18 x 10 cm (7 x 4 in). Mark a point
10 cm (4 in) up each long side.
Mark the centre of the top edge.
Draw lines from here to each of the
side points, and cut out. For the
roof: 2 rectangles 20 x 15 cm
(8 x 6 in).

1 Preheat the oven to 190°C/375°F/
Gas 5. Line several baking sheets
with baking parchment. Place the
syrup, treacle (molasses), sugar and
butter in a saucepan and heat gently,
stirring occasionally, until melted.

3 Roll out one-third of the dough
thinly, reserving the rest in a
polythene bag. Cut out two end walls.
Stamp out on each a window using a
2.5 cm (1 in) round cutter and a door
using a 2.5 cm (1 in) square cutter.
Place a sweet (candy) in each opening.
Bake for 8–10 minutes, then cool.

2 Sift the flour, ginger and
bicarbonate of soda (baking
soda) into a bowl. Add the yolks and
pour in the syrup mixture, stirring
with a wooden spoon. Knead on a
lightly floured surface until smooth.

4 Use the remaining dough to
make the two side walls and the
two roof pieces. Using the square
cutter, stamp out two windows in
each wall. Using the round cutter,
stamp out three windows in each
roof piece. Place sweets (candies) in
the openings and bake as before.

5 To decorate, pipe lines, loops and circles around the windows, doors and on the walls and roof with royal icing. Pipe beads of icing in groups of three all over the rest of the house and leave the pieces flat to dry.

6 To assemble the house, pipe icing along the side edges of the walls and stick them together to form a box shape on the cake board. Pipe a line of icing following the pitch of the roof on both end pieces and along the top of the roof pieces. Press gently in position and support while the icing sets. Pipe the finishing touches to the roof and base. Dust the cake board with icing sugar to look like snow. Wrap ribbon around the edges of the board.

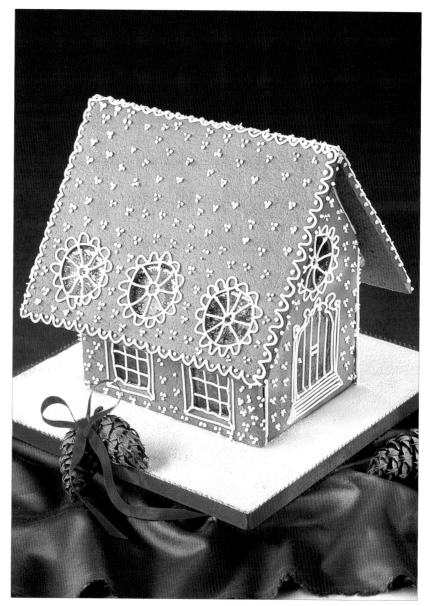

NOVELTY CHRISTMAS CAKES

*These individual cakes can be packed in their own little boxes
to make unusual gifts for children.*

MAKES 2 CAKES

*115 g (4 oz/1 cup) self-raising
(self-rising) flour
5 g (1 tsp) baking powder
(baking soda)
15 g (½ oz/1 tbsp) cocoa powder
115 g (4 oz/½ cup) caster
(superfine) sugar
115 g (4 oz/½ cup) soft margarine
2 eggs*

DECORATION

*45 ml (3 tbsp) apricot jam glaze
2 x 15 cm (6 in) round cake boards
350 g (12 oz) ready-to-roll icing
350 g (12 oz) white marzipan
food colourings
glitter flakes: white and red*

1 Preheat the oven to 160°C/325°F/
Gas 3. Grease and line two 15 cm
(6 in) round sandwich tins. Place all
the cake ingredients in a mixing bowl.
Mix together with a wooden spoon
and beat for 2–3 minutes.

3 Brush the apricot glaze over the
cakes and place them on the
cake boards. To make the clown, roll
out one-third of the icing to a round
large enough to cover one cake.
Smooth the icing over the cake and
trim at the base. Mould two ears and
press into position. Colour one-third
of the marzipan red and shape
a mouth and nose; reserve the
remainder. Colour a small piece of
marzipan black and roll out thin
lengths to outline the mouth and
make the eyes and eyebrows.

2 Divide the mixture between the
tins, smooth the tops and bake
in the oven for 20–25 minutes or
until the cakes spring back when
pressed in the centre. Allow to cool
on a wire rack. Remove the paper.

4 Colour another small piece
yellow and grate coarsely for the
hair. Colour another piece green for
the ruffle. Stick in position with
apricot glaze and sprinkle with white
glitter flakes.

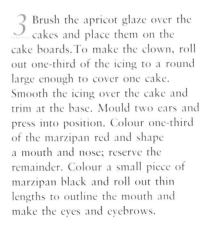

5 To make the Father Christmas
cake, colour the remaining
marzipan a skin tone using a tiny
amount of brown colouring and roll
out thinly to cover two-thirds of the
second cake. Trim. Roll out three-
quarters of the red marzipan thinly
and cover the remainder of the cake.
Gather the excess at one side to
make the hat. Mould a nose and
mouth from the remaining red
marzipan. Coarsely grate the
remaining white icing and use to trim
the hat and for the beard, moustache
and eyebrows. Gently shape grated
white icing into a small bobble for
the hat. Shape two black eyes and
press in position. Sprinkle red glitter
flakes on to the hat.

TIP

To make the apricot jam glaze, add
30 ml (2 tbsp) water to 45 ml
(3 tbsp) apricot jam in a small pan.
Heat gently, stirring, to melt the
jam, and sieve.

CREAMY CHRISTMAS FUDGE

A box of fudge in a selection of flavours makes a good alternative to a box of chocolates and is unfailingly popular. Arrange each layer in the box on a sheet of greaseproof paper, but there is no need to wrap the squares individually. The fudge will keep well for several weeks.

MAKES 900 G (2 LB)

50 g (2 oz/4 tbsp) unsalted (sweet)
butter, plus extra for greasing
450 g (1 lb/2 cups) granulated sugar
300 ml (½ pint/1 ¼ cups) double
(heavy) cream
150 ml (¼ pint/⅔ cup) milk
45 ml (3 tbsp) water
(this can be replaced with orange,
apricot or cherry brandy,
or strong coffee)

FLAVOURINGS

225 g (8 oz/1 cup) plain (semi-sweet)
or milk chocolate dots
115 g (4 oz/1 cup) chopped almonds,
hazelnuts, walnuts or brazil
nuts (optional)
115 g (4 oz/½ cup) chopped glacé
(candied) cherries, dates or
dried apricots (optional)
icing (confectioners') sugar

1 Butter a 20 cm (8 in) shallow square tin. Place the butter, sugar, cream, milk and water or other flavouring in a large heavy-based saucepan. Heat very gently, stirring occasionally with a wooden spoon, until all the sugar has dissolved.

3 For chocolate-flavoured fudge, add the chocolate at this stage. Remove from the heat and beat. Alternatively, add chopped nuts or fruit and beat until the mixture thickens and becomes opaque.

2 Bring the mixture to the boil and boil steadily, stirring only occasionally to prevent it from burning on the base of the saucepan. Boil until the fudge reaches just under soft ball stage (113°C/230°F for a soft fudge).

4 Pour the hot fudge into the prepared tin. Leave the mixture until cool and almost set. Using a sharp knife, mark the fudge into small squares. Leave in the tin until quite firm.

5 Turn the fudge out on to a board and invert. Using a long-bladed knife, cut into neat squares. You can dust some with icing (confectioners') sugar and drizzle others with melted chocolate if you wish.

TIP
A beautiful festive tin or gift box is the perfect finishing touch for this delicious gift.

CHOCOLATE TRUFFLES

*These rich fresh cream truffles will keep, well wrapped, for up to ten days
in the fridge. Serve them with after-dinner coffee, or arrange them in a lavish box
to make a sumptuous gift.*

MAKES 20–30

*175 ml (6 fl oz/¾ cup) double (heavy)
cream
275 g (10 oz) plain (semi-sweet)
chocolate, chopped
25 g (1 oz/2 tbsp) unsalted (sweet)
butter, cut into pieces
30–45 ml (2–3 tbsp) brandy (optional)
cocoa powder
finely chopped pistachio nuts
or hazelnuts*

VARIATION

To coat with chocolate, freeze the
truffles for at least 1 hour. Melt
400 g (14 oz) of dark, milk or
white chocolate, then allow to cool
slightly. Using a fork, dip each
frozen truffle into the cooled
chocolate, tapping the fork on the
edge of the bowl to shake off the
excess. Place on a baking sheet
lined with baking parchment and
chill at once.

1 Bring the cream to the boil in a
saucepan over a medium heat.
Remove from the heat and add the
chocolate, then stir until melted and
smooth. Stir in the butter and the
brandy, if using, then strain into a
bowl and leave to cool. Cover and
chill for 6–8 hours or overnight.

2 Line a large baking sheet with
greaseproof (wax) paper. Using
a small ice-cream scoop or two
teaspoons, form the chocolate mixture into 20–30 balls and place on
the paper. Chill again if the mixture
becomes too soft while you are
moulding the truffles.

3 To coat the truffles with cocoa,
sift the cocoa powder into a
small bowl, drop in the truffles one
at a time and roll to coat well,
keeping the round shape. To coat
with nuts, roll the truffles in finely
chopped nuts.

CHOCOLATE CHRISTMAS CUPS

These festive treats are a perfect way of using up Christmas pudding
left-overs. To crystallize cranberries, beat an egg white until frothy;
dip each berry in the egg white then in caster (superfine) sugar.
Place on sheets of baking parchment to dry.

MAKES 30–35 CUPS

275 g (10 oz) plain (semi-sweet)
chocolate, broken into pieces
70–80 foil or paper sweet
(candy) cases
175 g (6 oz) cooked, cold Christmas
pudding
75 ml (3 fl oz/⅓ cup) brandy or
whisky
chocolate holly leaves and crystallized
cranberries to decorate

1 Place the chocolate in a bowl over a pan of barely simmering water until it melts, stirring until smooth. Using a pastry brush, coat melted chocolate on to the inside of about 35 sweet (candy) cases. Allow to set, then apply a second coat, reheating the chocolate if necessary. Leave for 4–5 hours to set. Reserve the remaining chocolate.

2 Crumble the Christmas pudding into a small bowl. Sprinkle with brandy or whisky and allow to stand for 30–40 minutes, until the spirit (alcohol) has been absorbed by the pudding crumbs.

3 Spoon a little of the pudding mixture into each cup, smoothing the top. Reheat the remaining chocolate and spoon over the top of each cup to cover the surface right to the edge. Leave to set.

4 When the chocolate cups are completely set, carefully peel off the sweet cases and replace them with clean ones. Decorate with chocolate holly leaves and crystallized cranberries.

FESTIVE FLORENTINES

*These chewy ginger biscuits (cookies) are delicious served with ice cream
and are certain to disappear as soon as they are put on the table.*

MAKES 30

*50 g (2 oz/4 tbsp) butter
115 g (4 oz/8 tbsp) caster
(superfine) sugar
50 g (2 oz/¼ cup) mixed glacé
(candied) cherries, chopped
25 g (1 oz/2 rounded tbsp) candied
orange peel, chopped
50 g (2 oz/½ cup) flaked almonds
50 g (2 oz/½ cup) chopped walnuts
25 g (1 oz/1 tbsp) glacé (candied)
ginger, chopped
30 ml (2 tbsp) plain flour
2.5 ml (½ tsp) ground ginger*

TO FINISH
*50 g (2 oz) dark chocolate
50 g (2 oz) white chocolate*

TIP
To keep these florentines in good
condition, store them in an airtight
container.

1 Preheat the oven to 180°C/350°F/
Gas 4. Whisk the butter and
sugar together until they are light
and fluffy. Thoroughly mix in all
the remaining ingredients, except
the chocolate.

3 Remove the biscuits (cookies)
from the oven and flatten them
with a wet fork, shaping them into
neat rounds. Return to the oven for
3–4 minutes, until they are golden
brown. Let them cool on the baking
sheets for 2 minutes. Transfer them
to a wire rack to cool completely.

2 Cut baking parchment to fit your
baking sheets. Put four small
spoonfuls of the mixture on each
sheet, spacing them well to allow
for spreading. Flatten the biscuits
(cookies) and bake for 5 minutes.

4 Break the dark chocolate into
a bowl set over a pan of barely
simmering water to melt. Stir until
smooth. Spread the melted chocolate
on the undersides of half the biscuits
(cookies). Melt the white chocolate
and spread on the undersides of the
remaining biscuits (cookies).

CHRISTMAS COOKIES

Make these decorative cookies with any shape of biscuit (cookie) cutter.

MAKES ABOUT 12

75 g (3 oz/6 tbsp) butter
50 g (2 oz/generous ½ cup) icing
(confectioners') sugar
finely grated rind of 1 small lemon
1 egg yolk
175 g (6 oz/1 ½ cups) plain flour
pinch of salt

TO DECORATE
2 egg yolks
food colouring in red and green

TIP

For an alternative flavouring, omit the lemon rind and add 25 g (1 oz/⅓ cup) ground almonds and a few drops of almond essence (extract). Pack the cookies into an airtight tin to make a lovely, festive gift.

1 In a large bowl, beat the butter, sugar and lemon rind together until pale and fluffy. Beat in the egg yolk, and sift in the flour and the salt. Knead to form a smooth dough. Wrap in clear film (plastic wrap) and chill for 30 minutes.

3 Transfer the cookies to lightly greased baking trays. Mark the top of each one lightly with a 2.5 cm (1 in) holly-leaf cutter. Use a 5 mm (¼ in) plain piping nozzle to imprint the holly berries. Chill the biscuits for at least 10 minutes, until firm.

2 Preheat the oven to 190°C/375°F/ Gas 5. On a lightly floured surface, roll out the dough to 3 mm (⅛ in) thick. Using a 6 cm (2½ in) fluted cutter, stamp out the cookies, dipping the cutter in flour to stop it sticking to the dough.

4 Put each egg yolk into a cup. Mix red food colouring into one and green into the other. Paint the leaves and berries using a small paintbrush. Bake for 10–12 minutes, until the edges begin to colour. Let them cool slightly on the trays before transferring them to a wire rack.

CHOCOLATE NUT CLUSTERS

These delicious sweetmeats are very simple to make.

MAKES ABOUT 30

525 ml (18 fl oz/2 ¼ cups) double (heavy) cream
25 g (1 oz/2 tbsp) unsalted (sweet) butter, cut into small pieces
350 ml (12 fl oz/1 ½ cups) golden (corn) syrup
200 g (7 oz/1 cup) granulated sugar
90 g (3 ½ oz/½ cup) soft light brown sugar
pinch of salt
15 ml (1 tbsp) vanilla essence (extract)
425 g (15 oz/3 cups) hazelnuts, pecans, walnuts, brazil nuts, unsalted peanuts or a combination
400 g (14 oz) plain (semi-sweet) chocolate, chopped
25 g (1 oz/2 tbsp) white vegetable fat

TIP
If you do not possess a sugar thermometer, you can test for the "soft ball stage" by spooning a small amount of caramel into a bowl of cold water: it should form a soft ball when rolled between finger and thumb.

1 Lightly oil two baking sheets with vegetable oil. Cook the cream, butter, syrup, sugars and salt in a large, heavy-based saucepan over a medium heat until smooth, stirring occasionally. Bring to the boil and stir frequently until the caramel reaches 119°C/238°F (soft ball stage).

3 Chill the clusters for 30 minutes, until firm. Melt the chocolate and vegetable fat together in a medium saucepan over low heat, stirring until smooth. Cool slightly. Using a metal palette knife, transfer the clusters to a wire rack set over a baking sheet.

2 Plunge the bottom of the pan into a bowl of cold water to stop cooking. Cool slightly, then stir in the vanilla essence (extract). Stir in the nuts until well coated. Using an oiled tablespoon, drop spoonfuls of the mixture on to the prepared sheets, about 2.5 cm (1 in) apart.

4 Spoon chocolate over each cluster, being sure to cover it completely. Alternatively, use a fork to dip each cluster in the chocolate before returning it to the wire rack. Allow to set for 2 hours until hard. Store in an airtight container.

CHOCOLATE KISSES

Dusted with sugar, these rich biscuits (cookies) look attractive mixed together on a plate. Serve them with coffee, or as an accompaniment to ice cream.

MAKES 24

75 g (3 oz) plain (semi-sweet) chocolate, broken into pieces
75 g (3 oz) white chocolate, broken into pieces
115 g (4 oz/½ cup) butter
115 g (4 oz/8 tbsp) caster (superfine) sugar
2 eggs
225 g (8 oz/2 cups) plain flour
icing (confectioners') sugar, to decorate

1 Put each type of chocolate into separate small bowls and melt over a pan of barely simmering water. Set aside to cool.

2 Whisk the butter and caster (superfine) sugar until pale and fluffy. Beat in the eggs, one at a time. Sift in the flour and mix well.

3 Divide the mixture between the two bowls of chocolate. Mix each chocolate in thoroughly. Knead the doughs until smooth, wrap them in clear film (plastic wrap) and chill for 1 hour. Preheat the oven to 190°C/375°F/Gas 5.

4 Take up slightly rounded tea-spoonfuls of each dough and roll into balls in the palms of your hands. Arrange them on greased baking trays and bake for 10–12 minutes. Dust with sifted icing (confectioners') sugar and transfer to a wire rack to cool.

FRUITS IN LIQUEURS

Make these beautiful preserves when the fruits are in season and store them away to make luxurious Christmas gifts. Team them with rum, brandy, Kirsch or Cointreau.

MAKES 450 G (1 LB)

450 g (1 lb) fresh fruit such as apricots, clementines, kumquats, cherries, raspberries, peaches, plums or seedless grapes
225 g (8 oz/1 cup) granulated sugar
300 ml (½ pint/1¼ cups) water
150 ml (¼ pint/⅔ cup) liqueur or spirit (alcohol)

1 Wash the fruit. Halve and stone (pit) the apricots, plums and peaches. Prick kumquats, cherries and grapes all over with a cocktail stick (toothpick). Pare the rind from clementines, remove any white pith.

2 Place half the sugar in a saucepan with the water. Heat gently, stirring occasionally, until the sugar has dissolved. Bring to the boil. Add the fruit to the syrup and simmer gently for 1–2 minutes until the fruit is just tender but still whole.

3 Carefully remove the fruit using a slotted spoon and arrange neatly in warmed sterilized jars. Add the remaining sugar to the syrup in the pan and stir until it has dissolved completely.

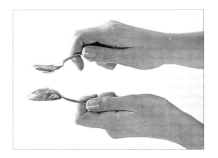

4 Boil the syrup rapidly until it reaches 107°C/225°F, or the thread stage. Test by pressing a small amount of syrup between two spoons: when they are pulled apart a thread should form. Allow to cool.

5 Measure the cooled syrup, then add an equal quantity of liqueur or spirit (alcohol) and mix together. Pour over the fruit until covered. Seal each jar, label and keep for up to four months.

CHRISTMAS CHUTNEY

*This chutney has a sweet but spicy flavour and makes the perfect
accompaniment to cold meats, pâtés and cheese. Instead of the fruits suggested,
you could use quince or rhubarb if you prefer.*

MAKES 1.75 KG (4–4½ LB)

450 g (1 lb/9) plums, stoned (pitted)
450 g (1 lb/6) pears, peeled and cored
225 g (8 oz/2) cooking apples, peeled
and cored
225 g (8 oz/4 sticks) celery
450 g (1 lb) onions, sliced
450 g (1 lb) tomatoes, skinned
115 g (4 oz/½ cup) raisins
15 g (½ oz/1 tbsp) grated fresh
root ginger
30 ml (2 tbsp) pickling spice
900 ml (1 ½ pints/3 ¼ cups)
cider vinegar
450 g (1 lb/2 cups) granulated sugar

1 Chop the plums, pears, apples,
celery and onions and cut the
tomatoes into quarters. Place all
these ingredients, together with
the raisins and ginger, in a very
large saucepan.

2 Wrap the pickling spice in
muslin and secure with string.
Add to the saucepan with half the
vinegar and bring to the boil. Cook
for about 2 hours, giving the mixture
an occasional stir.

3 Meanwhile, sterilize some jars
and plastic lids. When all the
ingredients are tender, stir in the
remaining vinegar and the sugar. Boil
until thick, remove the bag of spices
and fill each jar with chutney. Cover
with a wax paper disc and a lid.
Label when cold.

CRAB APPLE & LAVENDER JELLY

This fragrant jelly looks pretty with a sprig of fresh lavender suspended in the jar.

MAKES ABOUT 900 G (2 LB)

900 g (2 lb/5 cups) crab apples
1.75 litres (3 pints/7 ½ cups) water
lavender stems
900 g (2 lb/4 cups) granulated sugar

1 Cut the fruit into chunks and place in a preserving pan with the water and two lavender stems. Bring to the boil, cover the pan, and simmer very gently for 1 hour, stirring occasionally, until the fruit is pulpy.

2 Pour the contents of the pan slowly into a suspended sterilized jelly bag and leave to drip through slowly for several hours. Do not squeeze the bag or the jelly will become cloudy.

3 Discard the pulp and measure the quantity of juice in the bowl. To each 600 ml (1 pint/2½ cups) of juice, add 450 g (1 lb/2 cups) of sugar and pour into a clean pan. Sterilize the jars and lids required.

4 Heat the juice gently, stirring, until the sugar has dissolved. Bring to the boil and boil rapidly for 8–10 minutes until the setting point of 105°C/221°F is reached. Test this by putting a small amount of jelly on a cold plate. When cool, its surface should wrinkle when you push your finger through it.

5 Remove the pan from the heat and use a slotted spoon to remove froth from the surface. Carefully pour or ladle the jelly into a jug, then fill the warm sterilized jars. Quickly dip the lavender into boiling water and insert a stem into each jar. Cover with discs of waxed paper and seal.

SALMON PATE

Delicate fresh salmon pâté wrapped in slices of smoked salmon makes a luxurious
gift when packed in a pretty dish. Store the pâté in the fridge.

MAKES 4

350 g (12 oz) fresh salmon fillet
pinch of salt
freshly ground black pepper
15 g (½ oz/1 tbsp) chopped fresh dill,
plus sprigs to garnish
115 g (4 oz/4 slices) smoked salmon
115 g (4 oz/½ cup) curd or
cream cheese
75 g (3 oz/5 tbsp) unsalted (sweet)
butter
50 g (2 oz/1 cup) fresh white
breadcrumbs
5 ml (1 tsp) lemon juice
30 ml (2 tbsp) Madeira

1 Preheat the oven to 190°C/375°F/
Gas 5. Put the salmon fillet on a
large piece of greaseproof (wax)
paper placed on top of a sheet of
foil. Sprinkle with salt, pepper and
dill. Seal the foil and place on a
baking sheet. Bake for 10 minutes or
until just tender. Leave until cold and
remove the skin, saving any juices.

2 Cut out four pieces of smoked
salmon to fit the bases of four
individual ramekin dishes. Cut out
four more pieces the same size, to
cover the pâté, and reserve. From the
remaining smoked salmon, cut strips
to fit around the inside edges of each
dish. Cover the dishes and chill.

3 Place the cooked salmon and its
juices in a food processor with
the curd or cream cheese, butter,
breadcrumbs, lemon juice and
Madeira. Process until smooth.
Divide the mixture evenly between
the ramekin dishes and level the
surfaces. Cover with the reserved
smoked salmon and decorate with
sprigs of dill. Cover with clear film
(plastic wrap) and chill.

ANCHOVY SPREAD

This delicious spread has a concentrated flavour and is perfect on crisp toast.
Pack it into small jars to make attractive little gifts.

MAKES 600 ML (1 PINT/2½ CUPS)

2 x 50 g (2 oz) cans anchovy fillets,
in olive oil
4 garlic cloves, crushed
2 egg yolks
30 ml (2 tbsp) red wine vinegar
300 ml (½ pint/1¼ cups) olive oil
freshly ground black pepper
30 g (1¼ oz/2 tbsp) chopped
fresh basil
or thyme

1 Drain the oil from the anchovies and reserve. Place the anchovies and garlic in a food processor. Process until smooth. Add the egg yolks and vinegar, and process until the egg and vinegar have been absorbed by the anchovies.

2 Pour the olive oil into a measuring jug and add the reserved anchovy oil. Set the food processor to a low speed and add the oil, drop by drop, to the anchovy mixture until it is thick and smooth.

3 Add some freshly ground black pepper and fresh herbs, and blend until smooth. Spoon the mixture into small sterilized jars, cover and label. Store in the fridge.

PEPPERS IN OLIVE OIL

*The wonderful flavour and colour of these peppers will add
a Mediterranean theme to festive foods. Bottle the different coloured peppers
separately or mix them all together.*

*MAKES ENOUGH TO FILL THREE
450 G (1 LB) JARS*

*3 red peppers
3 yellow peppers
3 green peppers
300 ml (½ pint/1 ¼ cups) olive oil
pinch of salt
freshly ground black pepper
3 sprigs of thyme*

1 Prepare a hot grill or preheat the oven to 200°C/400°F/Gas 6. Put the whole peppers on a grill rack or baking sheet. Place under the grill or in the oven and cook for about 10 minutes until the skins are charred and blistered all over. Turn frequently during cooking.

2 Allow the peppers to cool for at least 5 minutes, then peel off the skins. Remove the cores, seeds and stalks. Slice each of the peppers thinly, keeping each colour separate, and place each in its own dish.

3 Pour one-third of the olive oil over each dish of peppers. Sprinkle with the salt and pepper and add a sprig of thyme to each dish. Stir to blend well. Sterilize three jars and lids and fill with peppers. Top up each jar with the oil. Seal and label.

TIP
Choose interesting jars that can be used again and again, long after the delicious contents have gone.

INDEX

Acknowledgements
The publishers would like to thank the
following people for designing and
making the projects in this book:
Fiona Barnett, Penny Boylan, Lynda
Burgess, Carole Clements, Sue Maggs,
Terence Moore, Janice Murfitt, Cheryl
Owen, Katherine Richmond, Deborah
Schneebeli-Morrell, Sally Walton, Stewart
Walton, Elizabeth Wolf-Cohen and
Dorothy Wood
Photographers:
Karl Adamson, Edward Allwright, John
Freeman, Michelle Garrett, Amanda
Heywood, Janine Hosegood, Debbie
Patterson, Steve Tanner

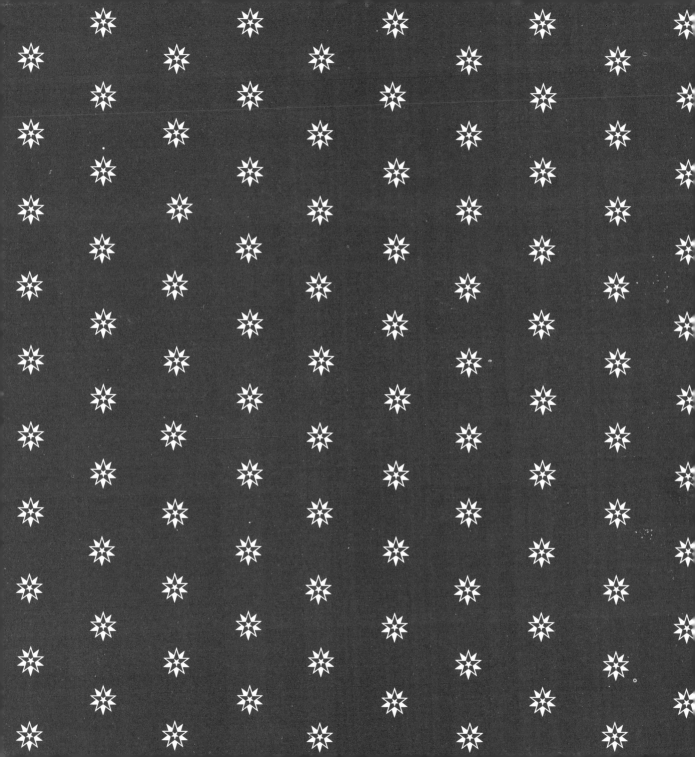